# Explorin

*A Comprehensive Naples Travel Guide 2023 to The Bustling Heart of Italy's Rich History, Culture, and Cuisine*

Willie F Smith

**Copyright 2023 © Willie F. Smith All rights reserved.**

No part of this book may be reproduced in any form or by any electronic or mechanical means, including information storage and retrieval systems, without permission in writing from the publisher, except by a reviewer who may quote brief passages in a review. This book is a work of non-fiction. The views and opinions expressed in this book are the author's own and do not necessarily reflect those of the publisher or any other person or organization. The information in this book is provided for educational and informational purposes only. It is not intended as a substitute for professional advice of any kind.

# Table of Contents

Table of Contents.................................................................. 3
Introduction............................................................................ 7
CHAPTER 1......................................................................... 11
Welcome to Naples............................................................ 11
    A Brief History of Naples............................................. 12
    Why Visit Naples............................................................ 12
    Neapolitan Culture and Traditions............................ 14
    Language and Customs................................................. 15
    Climate and Best Time to Visit................................... 16
    Transportation in Naples.............................................. 16
CHAPTER 2......................................................................... 19
Exploring Naples................................................................. 19
Historic Center: Heart of Naples.................................... 19
    Piazza del Plebiscito...................................................... 20
    The Royal Palace of Naples......................................... 23
    San Carlo Theater.......................................................... 27
    Galleria Umberto I......................................................... 31
    Castel Nuovo................................................................... 34
CHAPTER 3......................................................................... 40
Churches and Cathedrals................................................. 40
    Duomo di San Gennaro................................................ 40
    Basilica di Santa Chiara................................................ 44
    San Domenico Maggiore............................................. 47
    Gesù Nuovo Church...................................................... 50

**CHAPTER 4**................................................................ **55**
**Museums and Art Galleries**............................................. **55**
    Naples National Archaeological Museum................... 55
    Museo di Capodimonte................................................ 59
    Museo Cappella Sansevero...........................................62
    MADRE Contemporary Art Museum........................65

**CHAPTER 5**................................................................ **70**
**Neighborhoods and Districts**........................................... **70**
    Spaccanapoli................................................................ 70
    Quartieri Spagnoli....................................................... 74
    Vomero........................................................................78
    Chiaia.......................................................................... 82

**CHAPTER 6**................................................................ **86**
**Savory Delights: Neapolitan Cuisine**............................... **86**
    Classic Neapolitan Dishes............................................86
    Traditional Markets and Food Halls........................... 89
    Best Trattorias and Restaurants................................... 92

**CHAPTER 7**................................................................ **97**
**Beyond Naples: Day Trips and Excursions**................... **97**
    The Amalfi Coast........................................................ 97
    Pompeii and Herculaneum........................................101
    Mount Vesuvius........................................................ 105

**CHAPTER 8**.............................................................. **109**
**Practical Information and Tips**.................................... **109**
    Accommodation Options in Naples......................... 109
    Neighborhood Recommendations............................ 111

Getting Around Naples.................................................. 113
Safety Tips and Local Customs in Naples...................116
Local Customs and Useful Phrases............................ 117
Recommended Itineraries...........................................118
Festivals and Events..................................................... 119
**Conclusion..................................................................121**

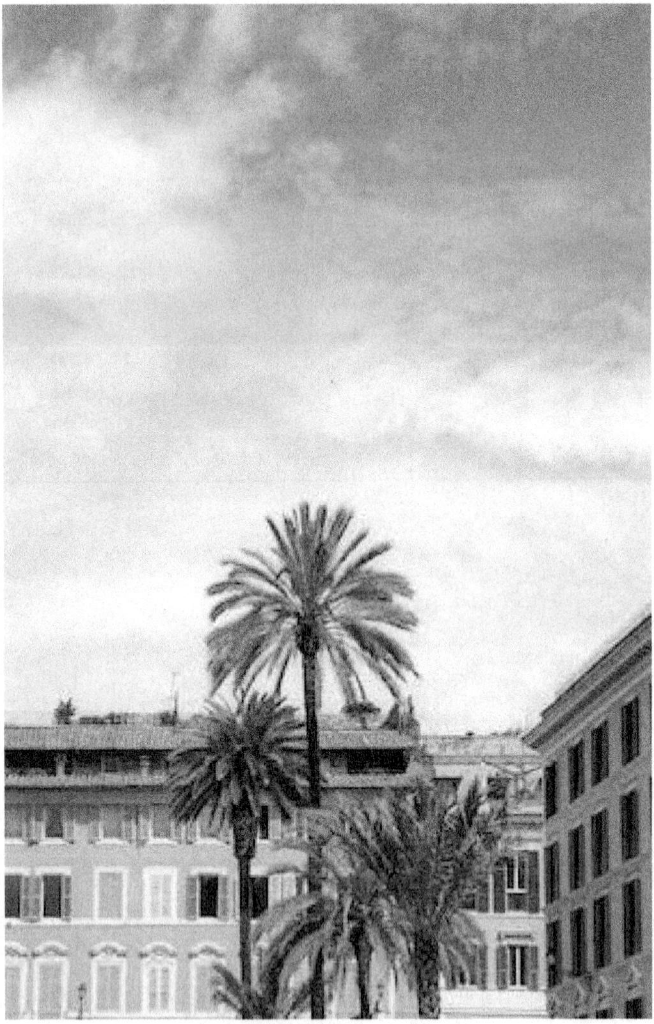

# Introduction

In the heart of the mesmerizing Italian peninsula, I embarked on an unforgettable journey to the bustling city of Naples. As I ventured through its ancient streets and gazed upon its magnificent landmarks, I found myself immersed in a world of unparalleled beauty and rich history.

My first steps led me to the historic center, a UNESCO World Heritage site, where the city's vibrant soul unfolded before my eyes. Wandering through narrow alleys lined with colorful buildings, I couldn't help but be captivated by the lively atmosphere that permeated every corner. The aroma of freshly baked pizza wafted through the air, enticing me to indulge in the city's renowned culinary delights.

Eager to uncover Naples' hidden treasures, I made my way to the captivating underground world of the Napoli Sotterranea. Descending into the depths of the city, I discovered a labyrinth of tunnels and chambers that revealed centuries of history. From ancient Roman aqueducts to secret catacombs, each step brought me closer to the city's intriguing past.

The allure of Naples continued to draw me towards its awe-inspiring landmarks. I found myself standing in awe before the imposing Castel dell'Ovo, perched majestically on the islet of Megaride. Legend has it that the castle's name, meaning "Egg Castle," originated from the belief that a magical egg hidden within its walls protected the city from destruction. The myth only added to the castle's mystical charm.

As the sun began to set, I followed the winding path leading up to the iconic hilltop fortress of Castel Sant'Elmo. From its vantage point, a breathtaking panoramic view unfolded before me. The Bay of Naples stretched out like a shimmering tapestry, framed by the majestic silhouette of Mount Vesuvius. It was a sight that left me breathless, reminding me of the city's proximity to the awe-inspiring natural wonders that surround it.

But it was not just the city's historical sites and natural beauty that mesmerized me. Naples' artistic legacy proved equally enchanting. The Museo di Capodimonte, with its impressive collection of Renaissance masterpieces, held me captive in its artistic embrace. Each stroke of the brush and chisel seemed to whisper tales of artistic genius and profound creativity.

Yet, amidst all the grandeur and history, it was the people of Naples who truly left an indelible mark on my heart. Warm and passionate, they embraced me with open arms, sharing stories and traditions that have been passed down through generations. From the lively street markets to the spirited conversations in cozy cafes, I experienced the true essence of Neapolitan culture—a celebration of life and community.

As my time in Naples drew to a close, I couldn't help but reflect on the profound impact this city had on me. It had awakened my sense of wonder and curiosity, opening my eyes to the beauty that lies beneath the surface of every place I visit. Naples, with its vibrant spirit, rich history, and warm-hearted people, had forever etched itself into the tapestry of my own personal exploration.

With a heavy heart, I bid farewell to this enchanting city, knowing that its beauty would forever be etched in my memory. Naples had taught me the art of exploration—the art of seeing beyond the obvious, delving into the depths of a place, and embracing the stories that unfold with each step. As I left the cobblestone streets behind, I carried with me the spirit of Naples, forever transformed by its wonder and discovery.

# CHAPTER 1

## Welcome to Naples

In the bustling heart of Italy's Campania region lies the captivating city of Naples, a place where ancient history, vibrant culture, and breathtaking landscapes converge. Nestled between the azure waters of the Tyrrhenian Sea and the towering presence of Mount Vesuvius, Naples boasts a rich heritage dating back centuries. As you step into its winding streets, you will be greeted by an atmosphere that is both chaotic and charming, pulsating with energy and authenticity.

# *A Brief History of Naples*

Naples, with its roots dating back to the ancient Greeks, holds a storied history that has shaped its identity and contributed to its cultural wealth. Founded as Neapolis in the 8th century BC, Naples became an important center of trade and culture in the Mediterranean. Over the centuries, it was ruled by various civilizations, including the Romans, Byzantines, Normans, and Spanish. This diverse historical heritage is evident in the city's architecture, art, and traditions, making Naples a captivating destination for history enthusiasts.

## *Why Visit Naples*

Naples is a city that captivates the senses and leaves a lasting impression on all who visit. Here are a few compelling reasons why Naples should be on your travel radar:

**Rich History:** Naples is a city steeped in history, having been founded by the Greeks in the 8th century BC. As the birthplace of the pizza and a prominent center of art and architecture, it has played a significant role in shaping Italian culture. From its ancient ruins and well-preserved archaeological sites to its splendid Renaissance palaces and churches, Naples is a treasure trove of historical wonders.

*Cultural Vibrancy:* Naples pulsates with a vibrant and distinct cultural identity. The city's passionate residents, known as Neapolitans, take great pride in their traditions, language, and culinary heritage. From the captivating strains of traditional Neapolitan music to the vibrant street art adorning its walls, Naples is a city where culture thrives and innovation blossoms.

*Culinary Delights:* Renowned worldwide for its mouthwatering cuisine, Naples offers a gastronomic adventure like no other. Indulge in authentic Neapolitan pizza, made with fresh local ingredients and baked to perfection in wood-fired ovens. Sample delectable seafood dishes, tantalizing pasta creations, and the famous sfogliatella pastries that will leave you craving for more. Naples is a food lover's paradise that promises to delight your taste buds.

*Natural Beauty:* Surrounding Naples are some of Italy's most stunning landscapes. The enchanting Amalfi Coast, with its cliffside towns and crystal-clear waters, beckons visitors to explore its breathtaking beauty. Mount Vesuvius, the infamous volcano that destroyed Pompeii and Herculaneum in

79 AD, stands as a reminder of the region's dramatic past. Nature lovers will find themselves immersed in awe-inspiring vistas and unforgettable experiences.

## *Neapolitan Culture and Traditions*

Neapolitan culture is a tapestry of traditions, customs, and vibrant expressions that define the city's unique character. Known for their warm hospitality, Neapolitans embrace a zest for life, love of music, and a deep-rooted passion for their city. The streets come alive with lively conversations, bustling markets, and vibrant festivals that celebrate the city's rich heritage. From the enchanting sounds of traditional Neapolitan music, such as the iconic song "O Sole Mio," to the spirited and colorful processions during religious festivals, Naples offers a cultural experience that is authentic and captivating.

## *Language and Customs*

The Neapolitan dialect, a variation of the Italian language, holds a special place in the hearts of the locals. While Italian is widely spoken and understood, you'll often hear Neapolitans conversing in their distinct dialect, which reflects the city's deep-rooted cultural identity. Don't be surprised to hear expressive hand gestures and a melodic rhythm accompanying their conversations. Learning a few basic Italian phrases and embracing the local customs will enhance your interactions and make your experience in Naples even more enjoyable.

## *Climate and Best Time to Visit*

Naples enjoys a delightful Mediterranean climate, characterized by mild winters and hot summers. The spring months of April to June and the fall months of September to October are considered the best times to visit, as the weather is pleasant and the tourist crowds are more manageable. During these seasons, you can explore the city comfortably and enjoy outdoor activities without extreme temperatures.

## *Transportation in Naples*

Navigating Naples is made easy with its efficient transportation system. The city offers an extensive network of buses, trams, and a metro system that connects various neighborhoods and attractions. The metro is particularly convenient for reaching popular sites such as the historic center and the archaeological museum. Taxis are readily available, and car rentals provide flexibility for exploring the city and venturing into the surrounding areas. However, keep in mind that driving in the city center can be challenging due to narrow streets and heavy traffic.

As you familiarize yourself with the history, culture, language, climate, and transportation options in Naples, you will be well-prepared to embark on your exploration of this captivating city. Get ready to immerse yourself in the rich tapestry of Naples' past, embrace the vibrant traditions, and discover the hidden treasures that await you around every corner.

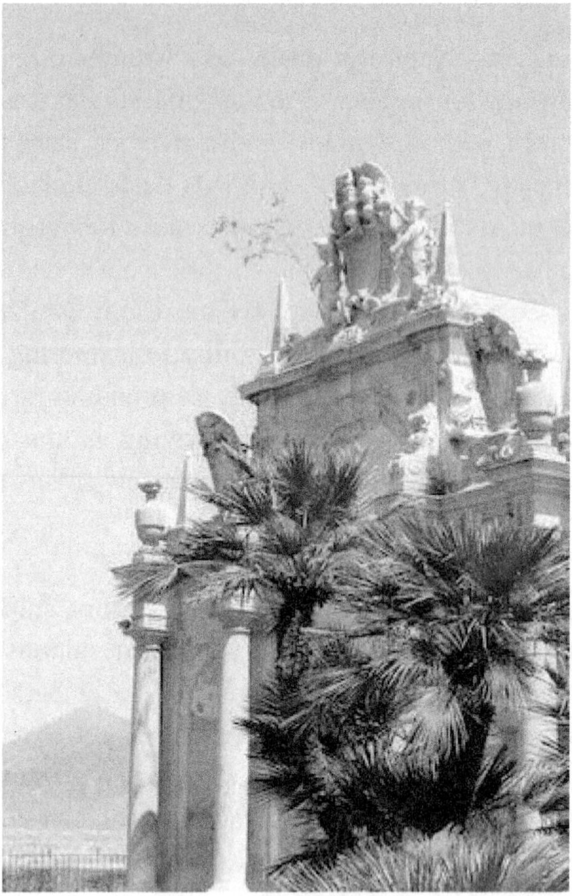

# CHAPTER 2

## Exploring Naples

---

## Historic Center: Heart of Naples

At the heart of Naples lies its historic center, a UNESCO World Heritage site that weaves together centuries of history, magnificent architecture, and vibrant street life. Step into this labyrinth of narrow alleys, known as "vicoli," and embark on a captivating journey through time.

## *Piazza del Plebiscito*

As you step into the grandeur of Piazza del Plebiscito, you are transported back in time to witness the rich tapestry of Naples' ancient civilization. This iconic square, situated at the heart of the historic center, stands as a testament to the city's enduring history, culture, and spirit.

Nestled between the Royal Palace of Naples and the Church of San Francesco di Paola, Piazza del Plebiscito occupies a prime location that has been at the center of Naples' social and political life for centuries. To reach this enchanting square, you can take a leisurely walk from other attractions in the historic center, or easily access it by public transportation, including buses and the Naples metro system.

The Piazza del Plebiscito holds deep social and cultural significance for the people of Naples. Its name, "Piazza del Plebiscito," stems from a pivotal moment in the city's history. In 1860, the residents of Naples voted in a plebiscite, a public vote, to determine whether they wished to be annexed to the newly formed Kingdom of Italy. The overwhelming majority voted in favor of unification, paving the way for Naples to become part of modern Italy. The square was later named to commemorate this pivotal event, celebrating the people's will and their collective aspiration for a united nation

Surrounded by awe-inspiring architectural marvels, Piazza del Plebiscito exudes grandeur and elegance. The most prominent structure is the Royal Palace of Naples, a magnificent building with a neoclassical façade and lavish interiors. The palace was once the residence of Bourbon monarchs and continues to serve as a symbol of Naples' royal heritage.

Another architectural gem adorning the square is the Church of San Francesco di Paola. This impressive domed church, inspired by the Roman Pantheon, showcases stunning neoclassical design and plays a significant role in the religious and cultural life of Naples.

## *The Majestic Obelisk and Fountain*

Dominating the center of Piazza del Plebiscito is the majestic obelisk of San Gennaro, a striking ancient Egyptian obelisk that was brought to Naples in the 19th century. It stands as a symbol of the city's deep historical connections and is a captivating sight, particularly when illuminated at night.

Adjacent to the obelisk, the Fontana del Nettuno (Fountain of Neptune) adds an elegant touch to the square. The fountain's statues of Neptune and mythical sea creatures pay homage to Naples' maritime heritage and underscore its significance as a vital Mediterranean port.

## *A Place for Gatherings and Celebrations*

Throughout history, Piazza del Plebiscito has been a focal point for various public gatherings, ceremonies, and celebrations. The square has hosted political rallies, religious processions, and cultural events, all of which have played a role in shaping the city's social fabric.

Even today, the Piazza del Plebiscito remains a vibrant center of activity. Locals and visitors alike gather here to bask in its beauty, enjoy leisurely walks, and soak in the ambiance of Naples' daily life.

As you explore Piazza del Plebiscito, you will feel the echoes of the past resonate through its majestic architecture and witness the vibrant pulse of modern Naples. This captivating square stands as a testament to the city's storied past, its unwavering spirit, and its enduring cultural legacy. Embrace the sense of timelessness that envelops you, and let Piazza del Plebiscito's enchanting aura become an unforgettable part of your Naples experience.

## The Royal Palace of Naples

Situated majestically on the vibrant Piazza del Plebiscito, The Royal Palace of Naples stands as a testament to the grandeur and opulence of Naples' royal past. This architectural masterpiece invites you to step into a world of regal splendor, where history comes alive and the echoes of ancient Naples civilization resound.

The Royal Palace of Naples enjoys a prime location at the eastern end of Piazza del Plebiscito, offering a commanding presence over the square. To reach this magnificent palace, you can take a leisurely stroll from other attractions in the historic center, as it is centrally located. Alternatively, various public transportation options, including buses and the Naples metro system, provide convenient access to the palace.

The Royal Palace of Naples holds immense social and cultural significance in the city's history. Constructed in the 17th century, it served as the primary residence for the Bourbon monarchs, who ruled over Naples and the Kingdom of the Two Sicilies. The palace played a pivotal role in the city's political and cultural life, serving as the seat of power and witnessing the ebb and flow of historical events that shaped Naples and its people.

As you step through the palace's magnificent entrance, you are transported to a bygone era of grandeur and refinement. The opulent interiors boast lavish decorations, ornate furnishings, and intricate frescoes, showcasing the artistic talents of renowned Italian craftsmen.

Explore the Royal Apartments, where you can marvel at the sumptuous rooms that once housed the royal family. Admire the intricate details of the Hall of Hercules, the grandeur of the Throne Room, and the elegance of the Court Theater, which was an important venue for cultural performances during the monarchy's reign.

## *Royal Collections and Treasures*

The Royal Palace of Naples is also home to an exceptional collection of art and historical artifacts. As you wander through the palace's galleries, you will encounter masterpieces by renowned artists, such as Titian, Caravaggio, and Luca Giordano. These works of art offer a glimpse into the cultural legacy of Naples and the patronage of the Bourbon monarchy.

Don't miss the opportunity to visit the Royal Chapel, a hidden gem within the palace, adorned with stunning frescoes and religious artwork. This sacred space provides a serene retreat, offering a glimpse into the spiritual aspects of royal life.

## *Witnessing History Unfold*

Beyond its architectural splendor and artistic treasures, The Royal Palace of Naples has witnessed pivotal moments in history. From political meetings and official ceremonies to royal weddings and diplomatic events, the palace's walls have borne witness to the rise and fall of dynasties, the forging of alliances, and the shaping of Naples' destiny.

Today, the palace continues to serve as a cultural institution, hosting exhibitions, concerts, and special events that showcase the rich heritage of Naples and its enduring connection to its royal past.

As you explore The Royal Palace of Naples, allow yourself to be captivated by the magnificence of its architecture, immerse yourself in the opulence of its interiors, and let the echoes of the past transport you to a time when Naples was a royal capital. This remarkable palace stands as a testament to the city's regal heritage, offering a captivating window into ancient Naples civilization and its enduring legacy.

## *San Carlo Theater*

Nestled in the heart of Naples' historic center, the San Carlo Theater stands as a testament to the city's rich cultural heritage and its deep-rooted love for the performing arts. Prepare to be enchanted as you delve into the captivating world of this illustrious theater, revealing its historical significance and the vibrant cultural tapestry it embodies.

Located adjacent to the grand Piazza del Plebiscito, the San Carlo Theater is conveniently situated for visitors exploring the historic center. You can easily reach the theater on foot from other attractions in the area. Alternatively, public transportation, such as buses and the Naples metro system, provides convenient access to the theater for those coming from different parts of the city.

The San Carlo Theater is one of the oldest and most prestigious opera houses in Europe, tracing its origins back to the 18th century. It holds a prominent place in Naples' social and cultural fabric, embodying the city's passion for music, opera, and the performing arts.

Throughout its long history, the theater has been a hub of artistic innovation and excellence. Countless renowned composers, conductors, and performers have graced its stage, leaving an indelible mark on the world of opera and music. The San Carlo Theater has served as a symbol of Naples' artistic legacy, attracting artists, musicians, and theater enthusiasts from around the globe.

As you approach the San Carlo Theater, you will be struck by its magnificent neoclassical façade, adorned with majestic columns and intricate details. Designed by renowned architect Antonio Niccolini, the theater's architecture reflects the grandeur and elegance of its time.

Step inside, and you'll find yourself in a splendid auditorium adorned with lavish decorations, ornate chandeliers, and plush red velvet seats. The theater's impeccable acoustics and intimate atmosphere create an immersive experience, allowing you to fully appreciate the magic unfolding on stage.

The San Carlo Theater has witnessed countless world premieres and performances of renowned operas, ballets, and symphonies. From iconic works by composers like Rossini, Verdi, and Mozart to innovative productions by contemporary artists, the theater has continuously pushed the boundaries of artistic expression.

Attending a performance at the San Carlo Theater is an unforgettable experience. Whether it's the passionate arias of an opera, the graceful movements of a ballet, or the soaring melodies of a symphony, each production captivates the audience, transporting them to a world of emotion and artistic brilliance.

Beyond its magnificent performances, the San Carlo Theater offers a glimpse into the behind-the-scenes magic of theater production. Take a guided tour to explore the backstage area, where you can witness the intricate sets, costume workshops, and rehearsal spaces. Gain insight into the dedication and craftsmanship that goes into creating a world-class production.

The San Carlo Theater's influence extends beyond its stage, reaching deep into the fabric of Naples' cultural landscape. It has nurtured generations of talented artists, providing a platform for local performers to showcase their skills and gain recognition. The theater's academy and training programs continue to foster the next generation of opera singers, musicians, and dancers, ensuring the preservation of Naples' cultural legacy.

As you immerse yourself in the world of the San Carlo Theater, you will be transported to a realm where music, drama, and art converge. Experience the power of a live performance, embrace the rich traditions of Naples' artistic heritage, and become a part of the living legacy that continues to unfold within the walls of this remarkable theater.

## *Galleria Umberto I*

Nestled in the heart of the historic center, Galleria Umberto I stands as a testament to the architectural and cultural legacy of Naples. This splendid shopping arcade, with its grandeur and elegance, invites you to step into a world of luxury and charm. explore the captivating allure of Galleria Umberto I, delving into its history, significance, and the vibrant life it breathes into ancient Naples civilization.

Galleria Umberto I is centrally located in the historic heart of Naples, making it easily accessible to visitors exploring the area. Situated just a short distance from other iconic landmarks, such as Piazza del Plebiscito and the Royal Palace of Naples, you can conveniently reach the gallery on foot. The city's efficient public transportation system, including buses and the Naples metro, also provide convenient access to the area.

Designed by renowned architect Emanuele Rocco, Galleria Umberto I was constructed in the late 19th century. The gallery's architectural style reflects the neoclassical and Art Nouveau influences of its time. Its soaring glass roof, elegant archways, and intricate ironwork create a harmonious blend of light, space, and decorative beauty.

As you enter the gallery, you'll be greeted by a sense of grandeur and sophistication. The arcade's spaciousness, adorned with marble floors and decorative elements, evokes a feeling of timeless elegance and sets the stage for a remarkable shopping and cultural experience.

Galleria Umberto I is not only a shopping arcade but also a cultural haven that encapsulates the essence of Naples' vibrant lifestyle. The gallery houses an array of luxurious boutiques, fashion houses, and specialty shops, offering a delightful shopping experience for those seeking high-end fashion, exquisite jewelry, and unique souvenirs.

Take a leisurely stroll along the gallery's promenades, and you'll discover cafés, restaurants, and pastry shops, where you can indulge in a cup of rich Neapolitan coffee or savor traditional delicacies. These establishments have become social hubs where locals and visitors gather to enjoy the vibrant ambiance and soak in the city's cultural energy.

Throughout history, Galleria Umberto I has been a favorite gathering spot for Naples' elite and intellectuals. It has served as a place for lively discussions, meetings, and encounters, fostering a sense of community and intellectual exchange. The gallery has witnessed the unfolding of Naples' social and cultural life, with its elegant spaces often hosting exhibitions, concerts, and other cultural events.

Galleria Umberto I holds a significant place in the identity of Naples. It symbolizes the city's aspirations for progress, its appreciation for artistic beauty, and its dedication to cultivating a sophisticated lifestyle. The gallery represents a fusion of commerce, art, and social interaction, reflecting the vibrant spirit and cultural heritage of Naples.

While Galleria Umberto I is deeply rooted in Naples' historical fabric, it continues to evolve and adapt to the changing times. Renovations have ensured its preservation, allowing visitors to experience its timeless beauty while enjoying modern amenities and contemporary offerings.

As you explore Galleria Umberto I, allow yourself to be enchanted by its architectural splendor, indulge in a world of luxury and refinement, and embrace the lively atmosphere that captures the essence of ancient Naples civilization. Experience the harmony of art, commerce, and culture that thrives within this magnificent arcade, and become a part of the ongoing legacy that Galleria Umberto I represents for the city of Naples.

## *Castel Nuovo*

Perched majestically on the city's waterfront, Castel Nuovo stands as a formidable testament to Naples' storied past. This iconic fortress, also known as Maschio Angioino, beckons you to explore its ancient walls and uncover the secrets of ancient Naples civilization. embark on a journey through time, delving into the historical significance and captivating allure of Castel Nuovo.

Castel Nuovo enjoys a prime location in the heart of Naples' historic center, overlooking the picturesque Gulf of Naples. Its strategic position makes it easily accessible for visitors exploring the area. You can reach the castle by walking from other attractions in the city center, as it is conveniently located. If you prefer public transportation, various buses and the Naples metro system provide convenient access to the castle.

Castel Nuovo has a rich and intriguing history that dates back to the 13th century. It was commissioned by Charles I of Anjou, a French monarch who conquered Naples, and subsequently became the residence and seat of power for various ruling dynasties. Over the centuries, the castle witnessed political intrigues, battles, and significant historical events that shaped the destiny of Naples.

As you approach Castel Nuovo, you will be greeted by its imposing façade and robust defensive walls. The castle's distinct architecture combines elements of medieval and Renaissance styles, showcasing the evolution of Naples' architectural heritage.

Step inside, and you will discover a treasure trove of historical and artistic wonders. The castle's courtyard, adorned with elegant arches and marble decorations, provides a captivating glimpse into the grandeur of its past. As you explore its various chambers, you will encounter impressive frescoes, intricate sculptures, and a collection of ancient artifacts, each offering a window into the rich cultural legacy of Naples.

One of the highlights of Castel Nuovo is the magnificent Triumphal Arch, a grand entrance adorned with intricate reliefs and statues. As you pass through this majestic gateway, you are transported into the heart of the castle.

Inside, you'll find the Angevin Hall, a majestic space that served as the throne room and ceremonial hall of the Angevin kings. Adorned with colorful frescoes depicting historical scenes and heraldic symbols, this hall exudes an aura of regal splendor and provides a captivating glimpse into the courtly life of ancient Naples.

Ascending to the top of Castel Nuovo, you'll reach the Maschio Tower, offering panoramic views of the city and the azure waters of the Gulf of Naples. From this vantage point, you can marvel at the sprawling cityscape and imagine the castle's strategic role in defending the city against invasions.

Adjacent to the tower, you'll find the Royal Chapel, a sacred space adorned with exquisite religious artwork and decorations. Step inside to witness the intricate details of its frescoes and sculptures, and experience the spiritual ambience that has touched the lives of countless visitors throughout the centuries.

Castel Nuovo not only serves as a historical monument but also as a vibrant cultural institution. Today, it hosts exhibitions, concerts, and cultural events that showcase the artistic talents of Naples and celebrate the city's rich heritage. The castle's walls reverberate with the echoes of ancient Naples civilization, inviting visitors to engage with the past and immerse themselves in the city's artistic and cultural tapestry.

As you explore Castel Nuovo, allow yourself to be transported to a time when knights roamed its halls, kings held court, and the fate of Naples hung in the balance. Experience the grandeur of its architecture, unravel the mysteries of its history, and become a part of the enduring legacy that Castel Nuovo represents for the city of Naples.

# CHAPTER 3

# Churches and Cathedrals

## *Duomo di San Gennaro*

The Duomo di San Gennaro is centrally located in the heart of Naples, making it easily accessible to visitors. Situated in the historic city center, you can reach the cathedral on foot from various attractions in the area. If you prefer public transportation, buses and the Naples metro system provide convenient access to the cathedral, with nearby stops just a short distance away.

The Duomo di San Gennaro is a place of deep religious significance for the people of Naples. It is dedicated to San Gennaro, the patron saint of the city, whose relics are preserved within the cathedral. The faithful flock to this sacred site to pay homage to the saint and seek his intercession.

The cathedral's origins can be traced back to the 13th century, although it has undergone numerous renovations and additions over the centuries. Its architectural style is a blend of Gothic, Renaissance, and Baroque elements, reflecting the evolving artistic tastes and influences of different eras.

Step inside the Duomo di San Gennaro, and you'll be awestruck by its beauty and grandeur. The interior is adorned with intricate frescoes, majestic domes, and ornate altars that showcase the craftsmanship of renowned artists and artisans.

One of the highlights of the cathedral is the Chapel of San Gennaro, where the saint's relics are enshrined. This chapel is a place of pilgrimage and devotion, where the faithful gather to witness the liquefaction of the saint's blood during special ceremonies.

Another notable feature is the Treasure of San Gennaro, a collection of precious artifacts and religious objects housed within the cathedral. This treasure includes exquisite gold and silver statues, reliquaries, and jewelry, many of which were donated by royalty and prominent figures over the centuries.

The Duomo di San Gennaro is not only a spiritual center but also a cultural symbol of Naples. It has witnessed countless historical events, royal ceremonies, and religious processions that have shaped the city's identity. The cathedral serves as a repository of Naples' cultural heritage, reflecting the fusion of art, religion, and history that characterizes the city.

One of the most significant events associated with the Duomo di San Gennaro is the Feast of San Gennaro, celebrated annually on September 19th. This vibrant festival attracts visitors from far and wide who come to witness the miracle of the liquefaction of the saint's blood.

The feast is a grand spectacle, featuring religious processions, street performances, and traditional rituals. It is a time of joy and devotion, as the people of Naples come together to honor their patron saint and celebrate their shared cultural heritage.

The Duomo di San Gennaro offers a window into the history of Naples, allowing visitors to connect with the city's ancient civilization. It is a place where the threads of faith, art, and tradition are interwoven, providing a profound and enriching experience for all who enter its sacred doors.

As you explore the Duomo di San Gennaro, let the reverence and beauty of the cathedral transport you to a realm where the spiritual and cultural heritage of ancient Naples converge. Experience the deep-rooted devotion, witness the artistry of centuries past, and become part of the ongoing legacy that this magnificent cathedral represents for the city of Naples.

## *Basilica di Santa Chiara*

The Basilica di Santa Chiara is located in the historic center of Naples, making it easily accessible to visitors. Situated near Piazza del Gesù Nuovo, it is within walking distance of many other attractions in the area. If you prefer public transportation, various buses and the Naples metro system provide convenient access to the basilica, with nearby stops just a short distance away.

As you approach the Basilica di Santa Chiara, you will be greeted by its iconic Gothic entrance and a sense of serene beauty that permeates the atmosphere. Step inside, and you'll discover the true essence of this remarkable site.

The basilica is renowned for its magnificent cloister, a peaceful haven adorned with delicate arches, vibrant frescoes, and an enchanting garden. The cloister is a sanctuary of serenity, where the harmonious interplay of light and shadow creates an ethereal ambiance that captivates visitors.
Within the Basilica di Santa Chiara lie the final resting places of Neapolitan royalty and nobility. Explore the chapels and tombs that line the walls, and you'll encounter the final resting places of illustrious figures from Naples' history. From Queen Sancha of Aragon to members of the Anjou and Bourbon dynasties, these tombs are a testament to the social hierarchy and noble lineage that shaped ancient Naples civilization.

The Basilica di Santa Chiara houses an impressive collection of artistic treasures that showcase the skills of renowned artists of the time. Admire the delicate majolica tiles that adorn the cloister, depicting biblical scenes and intricate patterns. Marvel at the exquisite frescoes that adorn the walls of the basilica, painted by some of the most talented artists of the Renaissance period.

One of the highlights is the famous Crucifix, attributed to the master sculptor Donatello. This remarkable artwork captivates viewers with its intricate details and emotional power, serving as a profound symbol of faith and redemption.

The Basilica di Santa Chiara holds great religious significance for the people of Naples. It is dedicated to Saint Clare of Assisi, a revered figure in the Catholic tradition known for her devotion and piety. The basilica stands as a place of pilgrimage and prayer, attracting believers from near and far who seek solace, spiritual guidance, and a connection to their religious roots.

Beyond its religious importance, the Basilica di Santa Chiara represents a cultural heritage that is deeply intertwined with the fabric of Naples. It serves as a testament to the city's artistic achievements, architectural prowess, and historical legacy. The basilica's rich tapestry of art and architecture tells the story of a bygone era, allowing visitors to connect with the vibrant cultural heritage of ancient Naples.

As you explore the Basilica di Santa Chiara, let the tranquility of its cloister envelop you, allowing the beauty of its art and the weight of its history to transport you to a time when faith and creativity flourished in the heart of this captivating city.

Experience the spiritual reverence, appreciate the artistic finesse, and embrace the cultural legacy that the basilica embodies, leaving you with a deeper appreciation of ancient Naples civilization.

## San Domenico Maggiore

San Domenico Maggiore is located in the heart of Naples, in the historic center of the city. Situated near Piazza San Domenico Maggiore, it is easily accessible by foot or public transportation. Various bus lines and the Naples metro system provide convenient access to the area, with nearby stops just a short distance away.

As you approach San Domenico Maggiore, you'll be immediately struck by its impressive Gothic façade, adorned with intricate details and exquisite sculptures. This architectural masterpiece dates back to the 13th century when it was built by the Dominican Order.

Step inside the church, and you'll be greeted by soaring arches, elegant columns, and a sense of awe-inspiring beauty. The interior showcases a harmonious blend of Gothic, Renaissance, and Baroque styles, reflecting the evolving architectural tastes of different periods in Naples' history.

San Domenico Maggiore has witnessed centuries of historical events, religious ceremonies, and cultural shifts. It served as a hub of intellectual and spiritual activity, attracting renowned theologians, scholars, and artists who shaped the cultural landscape of Naples.

The church has ties to some of Naples' most prominent historical figures, including the famous philosopher and theologian Thomas Aquinas, who resided in the adjacent monastery. It was also a site of political intrigue and power struggles, playing a significant role in the city's social and religious fabric.

Within the walls of San Domenico Maggiore, a treasure trove of artistic masterpieces awaits. Admire the stunning frescoes that adorn the chapel walls, depicting biblical scenes and saints. Marvel at the intricate woodwork of the choir stalls and the meticulously crafted altarpieces.

One of the highlights is the Chapel of San Gennaro, dedicated to the patron saint of Naples. It houses a venerated relic—a vial of San Gennaro's blood—which is believed to liquefy during special ceremonies, attracting throngs of faithful devotees.

San Domenico Maggiore is not only a place of worship but also a cultural symbol deeply intertwined with the identity of Naples. It has played a crucial role in preserving and promoting the city's artistic and intellectual heritage. Over the centuries, it has hosted concerts, exhibitions, and cultural events, fostering a vibrant artistic community and celebrating Naples' rich cultural legacy.

Today, the church continues to serve as a spiritual and cultural haven, welcoming visitors to explore its historical treasures and engage with the living legacy of ancient Naples civilization.

As you venture through the halls of San Domenico Maggiore, let the echoes of centuries past guide your steps. Feel the weight of history and the depth of faith as you immerse yourself in the art, architecture, and ambiance of this captivating church. Allow the stories and secrets of ancient Naples to unfold before your eyes, leaving you with a profound appreciation for the city's cultural heritage.

San Domenico Maggiore beckons you to discover the soul of Naples, where spirituality, art, and history converge in a mesmerizing tableau. Experience the timeless allure of this magnificent church and unravel the mysteries of ancient Naples civilization that reside within its sacred walls.

## *Gesù Nuovo Church*

Gesù Nuovo Church is located in the heart of Naples, in Piazza del Gesù Nuovo, making it easily accessible to visitors. Situated in the historic center of the city, it is within walking distance of many other notable attractions. Public transportation, including buses and the Naples metro system, provides convenient access to the area, with nearby stops just a short distance away.

As you approach Gesù Nuovo Church, you'll be immediately struck by its imposing facade, which blends elements of Gothic and Renaissance architectural styles. The church's exterior is characterized by its distinctive ashlar stone facade, adorned with ornate carvings and intricate details that hint at the splendor within.

Step inside, and you'll find yourself immersed in a sanctuary of awe-inspiring beauty. The interior features a breathtaking blend of architectural styles, including Baroque, Renaissance, and Neapolitan Gothic. Marvel at the intricate marble work, elegant columns, and soaring vaulted ceilings that create a sense of grandeur and reverence.

Gesù Nuovo Church has witnessed centuries of history, serving as a witness to the evolution of Naples and its people. Originally built as a palazzo for a noble family in the 15th century, it was later converted into a church by the Jesuits in the 16th century. The church played a significant role in the Counter-Reformation, a period of religious revival and reform in Europe.

Gesù Nuovo Church is not only a place of worship but also a repository of captivating stories and anecdotes. One of the most notable features of the church is the mysterious embedded iron mask in its facade. Legend has it that the mask was placed there to ward off evil spirits and protect the church from harm.

Another fascinating element is the Cappella di Sansevero, an annex to the church that houses the renowned sculpture "Veiled Christ" by Giuseppe Sanmartino. This masterpiece, known for its exquisite craftsmanship and lifelike depiction, continues to captivate visitors with its artistry and emotional impact.

Gesù Nuovo Church is not only an architectural gem but also a cultural symbol deeply rooted in the fabric of Naples. It has served as a center for spiritual devotion, a venue for artistic expression, and a meeting place for the community throughout history. The church has witnessed countless religious processions, ceremonies, and cultural events that have shaped the social and cultural landscape of Naples.

Today, Gesù Nuovo Church continues to be an active place of worship, drawing both locals and visitors seeking solace, inspiration, and a connection to the spiritual heritage of Naples.

As you explore Gesù Nuovo Church, allow yourself to be transported through time. Admire the stunning artworks, experience the spiritual ambiance, and contemplate the rich history that resonates within these sacred walls. Feel the presence of the countless individuals who have sought solace and found inspiration in this remarkable place.

Gesù Nuovo Church invites you to immerse yourself in the enchanting world of ancient Naples civilization, where spirituality, art, and history intertwine. Experience the profound beauty, cultural significance, and spiritual depth that this captivating church offers, leaving you with a profound appreciation for the rich tapestry of Naples' heritage.

Embark on this extraordinary journey through Gesù Nuovo Church, and let the stories and secrets of ancient Naples unfold before your eyes.

# CHAPTER 4

# Museums and Art Galleries

## Naples National Archaeological Museum

Naples National Archaeological Museum is centrally located in Naples, just a short distance from the historic center of the city. Situated in the Piazza Museo, it is easily accessible by foot, public transportation, or taxi. Various bus lines and the Naples metro system provide convenient access to the area, with nearby stops just a stone's throw away.

Step inside the Naples National Archaeological Museum, and you'll find yourself immersed in a world of wonder and discovery. The museum houses an extensive collection of artifacts from ancient Pompeii, Herculaneum, and other archaeological sites in the region, providing a unique window into the lives of the ancient inhabitants of Naples.

The museum itself holds historical significance as it was founded in the late 18th century by King Charles VII of Naples. Originally intended as a cavalry barracks, it was transformed into a museum to house the vast collection of antiquities unearthed in the excavations of Pompeii and Herculaneum.:

The Naples National Archaeological Museum is renowned for its exceptional collection of artifacts, each with its own story to tell. Marvel at the intricately detailed frescoes, mosaics, and sculptures that have survived the test of time. Admire the exquisite jewelry, pottery, and everyday objects that provide insights into the daily lives of ancient Naples civilization.

One of the museum's highlights is the Farnese Collection, which includes famous sculptures such as the Farnese Hercules and the Farnese Bull. These masterpieces of ancient art showcase the skill and craftsmanship of the artists of antiquity and offer a glimpse into the mythological narratives and cultural ideals of the time.

The Naples National Archaeological Museum holds immense social and cultural significance for both locals and visitors. It serves as a repository of Naples' rich history and a symbol of cultural identity. The museum not only preserves and showcases the artistic and archaeological heritage of the region but also fosters a deeper understanding and appreciation of ancient Naples civilization.

Through its exhibitions, educational programs, and research initiatives, the museum contributes to the preservation, interpretation, and dissemination of knowledge about ancient Naples. It serves as a bridge between the past and the present, connecting visitors to the vibrant cultural legacy that has shaped the city and its people.

As you explore the Naples National Archaeological Museum, be prepared to be transported back in time. Immerse yourself in the captivating narratives and intriguing mysteries of ancient Naples civilization. Allow the artifacts to speak to you, revealing the stories of the people who lived in this extraordinary region thousands of years ago.

The Naples National Archaeological Museum invites you to embark on a captivating journey of exploration and discovery. Delve into the depths of ancient history, and let the artifacts guide your imagination and spark your curiosity. Experience the profound cultural and historical significance of this remarkable museum, and leave with a newfound appreciation for the rich heritage of Naples.

Embark on this extraordinary adventure through the Naples National Archaeological Museum, and let the treasures of ancient Naples civilization come to life before your eyes.

## *Museo di Capodimonte*

Museo di Capodimonte is located on a hilltop in the Capodimonte Park, providing panoramic views of Naples. Situated just a few kilometers north of the city center, the museum can be easily reached by public transportation, taxi, or a leisurely stroll through the scenic park. Several bus lines connect the museum to the city center, making it a convenient destination for art enthusiasts and history buffs alike.

Museo di Capodimonte is housed in the magnificent Palazzo Reale di Capodimonte, a grand Bourbon palace built in the 18th century. The palace itself is a work of art, boasting elegant architecture and spacious rooms that provide the perfect backdrop for the museum's extensive collection.

The museum is renowned for its vast collection of artworks, spanning various periods and styles. Admire the masterpieces of Italian Renaissance and Baroque art, including works by renowned artists such as Caravaggio, Titian, Raphael, and Botticelli. Marvel at the exquisite sculptures, intricate tapestries, and decorative arts that adorn the museum's galleries.

One of the highlights of Museo di Capodimonte is the Farnese Collection, acquired by the Bourbon rulers of Naples in the 18th century. This collection includes ancient Roman sculptures, classical artifacts, and an impressive array of Renaissance and Baroque paintings. The Farnese marbles, in particular, are a sight to behold, with their intricate details and remarkable craftsmanship.

Museo di Capodimonte holds immense social and cultural significance for Naples and its people. It not only preserves and showcases extraordinary artworks but also serves as a symbol of the city's artistic and cultural heritage. The museum has played a vital role in promoting art education, research, and cultural exchange.

Through its exhibitions, educational programs, and collaborations with international institutions, Museo di Capodimonte enriches the cultural landscape of Naples and fosters a deeper understanding and appreciation of art. It provides a platform for visitors to engage with the rich artistic legacy of ancient Naples civilization and its influence on the wider art world.

As you explore Museo di Capodimonte, prepare to be captivated by the beauty and depth of the artworks that grace its galleries. Immerse yourself in the narratives and emotions conveyed by each brushstroke and sculpture. Allow the art to transport you through time, offering glimpses into the past and inspiring new perspectives.

Museo di Capodimonte invites you to embark on a journey of aesthetics and contemplation. Wander through the museum's halls, discover hidden gems, and connect with the artistic expressions of ancient Naples civilization. Let the art guide your imagination, evoke your emotions, and leave a lasting impression on your cultural journey.

Embark on this extraordinary adventure through Museo di Capodimonte, and let the power of art and culture touch your soul in profound and meaningful ways.

## *Museo Cappella Sansevero*

Museo Cappella Sansevero is located in the historic center of Naples, near the vibrant neighborhood of Spaccanapoli. Situated on Via Francesco De Sanctis, the museum is easily accessible by foot, public transportation, or taxi. Several bus and tram lines pass through the area, making it convenient for visitors to reach the museum.

Museo Cappella Sansevero is housed within the Chapel of Sansevero, a small chapel that dates back to the 16th century. This enigmatic museum is renowned for its unique collection of artworks, which blend artistry and mysticism in a captivating manner.

One of the most famous and intriguing works housed in Museo Cappella Sansevero is the Veiled Christ (Cristo Velato) by Giuseppe Sanmartino. This breathtaking sculpture depicts the figure of Christ lying under a sheer marble veil, revealing intricate details of his body beneath. The Veiled

Christ is not only a masterful display of artistry but also a symbol of the profound spiritual beliefs and devotion of the people of Naples.

Within the museum, you will also find a collection of anatomical sculptures created by the renowned 18th-century artist Giuseppe Salerno. These intricately carved figures showcase the delicate nature of the human body, reflecting the scientific and artistic pursuits of the time. The anatomical sculptures are a testament to the intellectual curiosity and exploration of Naples during the Renaissance.

Museo Cappella Sansevero holds significant social and cultural value for the people of Naples. It represents a unique blend of art, spirituality, and intellectual curiosity that has been deeply ingrained in the city's cultural fabric for centuries. The museum offers visitors a glimpse into the profound religious devotion and artistic excellence of ancient Naples civilization.

The chapel and its artworks have long been shrouded in mystery and legends. Tales of secret alchemical experiments and mystical practices have surrounded the chapel, adding an air of intrigue to the museum. Museo Cappella Sansevero has become not only a cultural institution but also a place that sparks imagination and fuels curiosity, inviting visitors to delve deeper into the enigmatic history of Naples.

As you explore Museo Cappella Sansevero, prepare to be captivated by the ethereal beauty and symbolism of the artworks. Marvel at the intricate marble sculptures, admire the delicate details, and ponder the deeper meanings they convey. Allow the mysterious atmosphere of the chapel to transport you to a different time, evoking a sense of wonder and fascination.

Museo Cappella Sansevero invites you on a journey of discovery, where art, history, and spirituality intertwine. Experience the allure of this hidden gem, and let the artistic masterpieces and enigmatic stories unfold before your eyes. Immerse yourself in the captivating world of Museo Cappella Sansevero and leave with a newfound appreciation for the artistic legacy and mystical traditions of ancient Naples civilization.

Embark on this extraordinary adventure through Museo Cappella Sansevero, and let the art and mystery of Naples captivate your senses and ignite your imagination.

# MADRE Contemporary Art Museum

MADRE Contemporary Art Museum is situated in the historic center of Naples, near the renowned Piazza Bellini. Located on Via Luigi Settembrini, the museum enjoys a prime location that is easily accessible by public transportation, taxi, or a leisurely stroll through the charming streets of Naples. Several bus and metro lines connect the museum to various parts of the city, making it convenient for visitors to reach their destination.

MADRE Contemporary Art Museum is housed in a renovated 19th-century building that seamlessly blends the old and the new. Its modern and minimalist design creates a striking contrast against the surrounding historic architecture, reflecting the progressive nature of contemporary art. The museum serves as a platform for both established and emerging artists, showcasing a diverse range of artistic expressions.

The museum's collection boasts an impressive array of contemporary artworks, including paintings, sculptures, installations, multimedia pieces, and more. Visitors can witness the evolution of artistic practices and engage with thought-provoking creations that push the boundaries of traditional art forms.

MADRE Contemporary Art Museum places a strong emphasis on the social and cultural significance of art, addressing relevant themes and sparking meaningful dialogues. The exhibitions often tackle pressing issues of our time, encouraging visitors to reflect on society, politics, identity, and the human experience.

MADRE Contemporary Art Museum plays a vital role in shaping the cultural landscape of Naples and beyond. It acts as a catalyst for artistic experimentation, innovation, and dialogue. The museum actively engages with the local community through educational programs, workshops, and outreach initiatives, fostering a deeper understanding and appreciation of contemporary art.

Moreover, MADRE Contemporary Art Museum serves as a platform for the creative voices of Naples, providing artists with opportunities to showcase their work and gain international recognition. It acts as a bridge between local and global art scenes, creating a vibrant exchange of ideas and perspectives.

Ancient Naples civilization has a rich history of artistic expression and cultural heritage. MADRE Contemporary Art Museum represents a continuation of this legacy, demonstrating that Naples remains a hub of creativity and artistic excellence.

As you explore MADRE Contemporary Art Museum, be prepared to have your senses awakened and your perspectives challenged. Encounter artworks that evoke emotions, provoke thoughts, and invite introspection. Engage with interactive installations that blur the boundaries between the observer and the art itself.

MADRE Contemporary Art Museum offers a space for contemplation, exploration, and inspiration. Its thought-provoking exhibitions and dynamic programming create an immersive experience that invites visitors to actively participate in the artistic journey.

Embark on this extraordinary adventure through MADRE Contemporary Art Museum, and let the power of contemporary art ignite your imagination and broaden your horizons. Discover the ever-evolving nature of artistic expression, embrace the diversity of perspectives, and witness the transformative potential of art.

MADRE Contemporary Art Museum invites you to be part of the dynamic dialogue between art and society, leaving you with a renewed appreciation for the cultural richness and artistic vitality of ancient Naples civilization.

# CHAPTER 5

## Neighborhoods and Districts

### *Spaccanapoli*

Spaccanapoli is located in the historic center of Naples, Italy. Its name, which translates to "Naples splitter," aptly describes its geographical position as the main street that divides the city into two halves. Spanning approximately two kilometers, this iconic street is lined with narrow alleys, colorful facades, and an abundance of local shops, restaurants, and cultural sites.

To reach Spaccanapoli, you can easily navigate through the city center on foot. It is accessible from various points, including the nearby Naples Central Station and the popular Piazza del Gesù Nuovo. Additionally, public transportation options, such as buses and trams, provide convenient access to the neighborhood.

Stepping into Spaccanapoli is like entering a time capsule that transports you back to the ancient origins of Naples. This historic neighborhood is characterized by its winding streets, vibrant atmosphere, and unique architectural features. As you wander through its narrow alleys, you'll encounter centuries-old buildings adorned with ornate balconies and picturesque courtyards.

The soul of Naples truly comes to life in Spaccanapoli. Its bustling streets are filled with the energetic chatter of locals going about their daily routines, craftsmen perfecting their art, and street vendors selling mouth-watering Neapolitan specialties. The neighborhood exudes a lively and authentic ambiance that captivates visitors and allows them to experience the essence of Naples.

Spaccanapoli holds great historical and cultural significance. It traces its roots back to the ancient Greek and Roman periods when the city of Neapolis was established. Over the centuries, the neighborhood has witnessed the rise and fall of empires, the influence of different cultures, and the development of the city.

Through its narrow streets and hidden corners, Spaccanapoli reveals glimpses of Naples' rich past. From medieval churches and palaces to ancient Roman ruins, the neighborhood is a living testament to the city's historical legacy. Each corner has a story to tell, and every building carries the echoes of the past.

Spaccanapoli is not only a place of historical importance but also a vibrant hub of social and cultural activity. It is a melting pot of traditions, customs, and artistry that define the unique character of Naples. The neighborhood's authenticity and local charm attract artists, artisans, and performers, contributing to the vibrant cultural scene of the city.

As you explore Spaccanapoli, you'll discover hidden treasures, such as artisan workshops, traditional music performances, and local artisans preserving ancient crafts. The neighborhood serves as a platform for cultural exchange and artistic expression, fostering a sense of community and preserving the intangible heritage of Naples.

Spaccanapoli offers a captivating glimpse into the spirit of ancient Naples civilization. Its narrow streets and vibrant energy reflect the resilience, creativity, and warmth of the Neapolitan people. The district's authenticity, cultural richness, and historical significance make it an essential destination for those seeking to uncover the soul of Naples.

Embark on this enchanting journey through Spaccanapoli, and let the labyrinthine streets guide you through the heart of Naples. Engage with the locals, savor traditional cuisine, and immerse yourself in the vibrant atmosphere that encapsulates the essence of this ancient city.

Spaccanapoli beckons you to explore its hidden corners, discover its stories, and embrace the enchantment of ancient Naples civilization. Get ready to create lasting memories and experience the true soul of Naples in this remarkable neighborhood.

## *Quartieri Spagnoli*

Quartieri Spagnoli, also known as the Spanish Quarters, is nestled in the heart of Naples, Italy. This neighborhood stretches between the historic center and the Vomero hill, creating a vibrant hub of local life and cultural activity. Its narrow streets, colorful buildings, and bustling atmosphere embody the authentic spirit of Naples.

To reach Quartieri Spagnoli, you can start from the historic center of Naples, near popular landmarks such as Piazza del Plebiscito or Castel Nuovo. From there, you can walk or take public transportation, such as buses or trams, to reach the neighborhood. As you venture into Quartieri Spagnoli, be prepared for an immersive experience that will transport you back in time.

Stepping into Quartieri Spagnoli is like entering a different world within the vibrant city of Naples. This neighborhood is characterized by its maze-like streets, tightly packed buildings, and lively atmosphere. As you navigate through its alleys, you'll be greeted by vibrant street life, local vendors selling fresh produce, and the aroma of delicious Neapolitan cuisine.

Quartieri Spagnoli is best explored on foot, allowing you to soak in the authentic ambiance and discover hidden gems along the way. The narrow streets, known as "vici," are adorned with vibrant laundry hanging between buildings, colorful street art, and the occasional glimpse of a local nonna peering out from a balcony. Embrace the energy of the neighborhood and let its charm captivate you.

Quartieri Spagnoli has a rich historical background that dates back centuries. Its name, Spanish Quarters, originates from the Spanish presence in Naples during the 16th and 17th centuries. The neighborhood was initially built to house the Spanish garrison and their families, and it has retained its distinctive character throughout the years.

This neighborhood has witnessed the ebb and flow of history, from the Spanish influence to the French occupation and the unification of Italy. Quartieri Spagnoli has evolved into a symbol of resilience and community, with its unique blend of cultures and traditions contributing to the cultural tapestry of Naples.

Quartieri Spagnoli is not just a residential area but also a vibrant cultural hub that reflects the true spirit of Naples. It is a place where traditions are upheld, and the local community thrives. The neighborhood's social fabric is woven together by the close-knit relationships among its residents, known as "spagnoli," who take pride in their distinct identity.

The lively streets of Quartieri Spagnoli are a testament to the neighborhood's vibrant social life. It is common to see locals engaging in animated conversations, children playing soccer in narrow alleys, and families gathering at piazzas for social events. The neighborhood also boasts a lively market scene, where you can find an array of fresh produce, spices, and traditional products.

Quartieri Spagnoli encapsulates the authentic essence of Naples, where traditions, community, and a strong sense of identity converge. It is a place where you can immerse yourself in the local way of life, interact with the friendly residents, and experience the warmth and hospitality for which Naples is renowned.

Quartieri Spagnoli offers a captivating glimpse into the ancient civilization of Naples. Its streets, buildings, and local traditions serve as a living testimony to the city's historical roots. As you explore this neighborhood, you'll discover remnants of ancient architecture, hidden chapels, and cultural practices that have been preserved through generations.

One fascinating anecdote is the presence of ancient Greek walls that lie beneath the surface of Quartieri Spagnoli. These archaeological remains are a reminder of the city's Greek origins and offer a glimpse into its early history. Walking through the neighborhood, you can't help but feel the weight of centuries of civilization that have shaped the city of Naples.

In conclusion, Quartieri Spagnoli is a neighborhood that encapsulates the vibrant essence of Naples. It invites you to delve into its streets, embrace its traditions, and connect with its warm-hearted residents. By exploring Quartieri Spagnoli, you will not only experience the social and cultural significance of this captivating district but also gain a deeper appreciation for the ancient Naples civilization that continues to thrive within its boundaries.

## *Vomero*

Vomero is located on the hillside in the western part of Naples, offering breathtaking views of the city, the Bay of Naples, and the iconic Mount Vesuvius. To reach Vomero, you can take various means of transportation depending on your starting point.

From the historic center of Naples, you can take the funicular railway, a unique mode of transport that will elevate your experience as you ascend the hill to Vomero. The funicular departs from the

Montesanto station and takes you directly to Piazza Vanvitelli, the heart of Vomero. Alternatively, you can take a taxi, bus, or even enjoy a leisurely stroll if you're up for the challenge.

Vomero is a neighborhood that effortlessly combines history, culture, and modernity. It is home to elegant residential buildings, bustling commercial streets, and charming squares that create a vibrant atmosphere. As you wander through its streets, you'll encounter a variety of shops, cafes, and restaurants, where you can indulge in local delicacies and soak in the lively ambiance.

One of the main attractions in Vomero is Castel Sant'Elmo, a medieval fortress that offers panoramic views of the city and the surrounding area. This historic landmark stands as a testament to the city's rich past and serves as a cultural hub, hosting exhibitions, events, and performances.

Vomero has long been considered a prestigious neighborhood, attracting affluent residents, artists, and intellectuals. Its elegant architecture, tree-lined streets, and vibrant cultural scene have made it a center of social and cultural life in Naples.

The neighborhood is also known for its educational institutions, including the prestigious University of

Naples Federico II, which has a campus in Vomero. This presence of academic institutions further contributes to the neighborhood's intellectual and cultural vibrancy.

Vomero is a hub of artistic expression, with several art galleries, theaters, and cultural centers scattered throughout the area. It is not uncommon to stumble upon art exhibitions, live performances, or literary events that showcase the creative talent that thrives in Vomero.

Vomero has a rich historical background that dates back centuries. The neighborhood's name is believed to originate from the Latin word "Vomerium," meaning plowshare, possibly referencing the agricultural use of the area in ancient times.

Throughout history, Vomero has witnessed significant events and has been home to influential figures. It played a role in the Norman and Angevin periods, and its strategic location made it a site of military importance. Today, traces of its historical significance can still be seen in the form of ancient churches, palaces, and architectural elements that dot the neighborhood.

Vomero offers a captivating glimpse into ancient Naples civilization. Its location on a hill provided a vantage point for observing and defending the city. The strategic position of Vomero made it an attractive settlement for various civilizations throughout history, including the Greeks, Romans, and Normans.

One fascinating anecdote is the presence of underground tunnels that connect Vomero to the historic center of Naples. These tunnels, known as "Borbonic tunnels," were originally built as escape routes for the Bourbon royal family during times of unrest. Exploring these hidden passages unveils the secrets of the past and transports you to a different era.

Vomero is a neighborhood that embodies the captivating aspects of ancient Naples civilization. Its elevated location, cultural attractions, and historical significance make it a must-visit destination for anyone seeking to delve into the rich heritage of Naples. By exploring Vomero, you will not only be rewarded with panoramic views and cultural experiences but also gain a deeper appreciation for the enduring spirit of ancient Naples that continues to thrive in this captivating neighborhood.

# Chiaia

Chiaia is located in the western part of Naples, adjacent to the historic center and overlooking the Bay of Naples. Its prime location along the coastline makes it easily accessible from various parts of the city.

To reach Chiaia, you can take advantage of the city's efficient public transportation system. The Toledo metro station, which is one of the most beautiful metro stations in the world, provides a convenient entry point to the neighborhood. From there, you can walk or take a short bus ride to Chiaia.

Chiaia is known for its elegant atmosphere, tree-lined streets, and stunning views of the bay. The neighborhood is a popular destination for both locals and visitors, offering a wide range of experiences to indulge in.

One of the highlights of Chiaia is the picturesque waterfront promenade known as Lungomare Caracciolo. This scenic walkway stretches along the coastline, offering breathtaking views of the bay, Mount Vesuvius, and the enchanting Castel dell'Ovo. Taking a leisurely stroll along Lungomare Caracciolo allows you to soak in the beauty of the sea and enjoy the vibrant atmosphere of Chiaia.

Chiaia has long been considered a prestigious neighborhood, attracting the affluent and intellectual elite of Naples. Its elegant buildings, upscale boutiques, and high-end restaurants create an ambiance of sophistication.

The neighborhood is also known for its vibrant cultural scene. Chiaia is home to the prestigious Teatro di San Carlo, one of the oldest and most renowned opera houses in the world. Attending a performance at this historic theater is a must for any art lover visiting Naples.

In addition to the theater, Chiaia hosts a variety of cultural events, including art exhibitions, music festivals, and literary gatherings. The neighborhood's vibrant cultural calendar reflects the city's rich artistic heritage and provides a platform for local and international talents to showcase their work.

Chiaia has a fascinating historical background that dates back centuries. The name "Chiaia" is derived from the Greek word "khaià," meaning "coastal area." This reflects the neighborhood's ancient roots and its connection to the Greek colonization of Naples.

Throughout history, Chiaia has been a sought-after residential area for the aristocracy and the bourgeoisie. Its prime location, with its proximity to the sea and the abundance of natural beauty, made it a desirable place to live.

Chiaia provides a captivating glimpse into the ancient Naples civilization. The neighborhood's coastal location and its historical significance as a port city reflect the importance of maritime trade and the influence of different cultures on Naples throughout history.

One fascinating anecdote is the presence of underwater archaeological sites off the coast of Chiaia. These submerged ruins hold remnants of ancient structures, pottery, and artifacts, shedding light on the ancient maritime activities and trade networks that thrived in the region.

Chiaia is a neighborhood that offers a captivating blend of elegance, natural beauty, and cultural richness. By exploring Chiaia, you will not only be immersed in the social and cultural significance of this captivating district but also gain a deeper appreciation for the ancient Naples civilization that continues to leave its mark on the city.

# CHAPTER 6

## Savory Delights: Neapolitan Cuisine

Neapolitan cuisine is renowned worldwide for its rich flavors, fresh ingredients, and deep-rooted culinary traditions. The food culture of Naples reflects the city's vibrant history, with influences from Greek, Roman, Spanish, and French cuisines. From mouthwatering pizzas to delectable pasta dishes and delightful pastries, Neapolitan cuisine offers a gastronomic experience like no other.

### *Classic Neapolitan Dishes*

***Neapolitan Pizza***

Neapolitan pizza holds a special place in the hearts of food enthusiasts. It originated in Naples and is characterized by its thin, soft crust and simple yet flavorful toppings. The traditional Neapolitan pizza, known as "Pizza Margherita," features San Marzano tomatoes, mozzarella cheese, fresh basil leaves, and a drizzle of extra virgin olive oil. It is cooked in a wood-fired oven, resulting in a deliciously crispy and chewy crust.

## *Pasta alla Genovese*

Pasta alla Genovese is a classic Neapolitan pasta dish that exemplifies the region's love for hearty flavors. It consists of pasta (usually rigatoni or ziti) served with a slow-cooked sauce made from onions, beef, and aromatic herbs. The sauce develops a rich and sweet flavor through the long cooking process, resulting in a comforting and satisfying dish.

## *Mozzarella di Bufala*

Mozzarella di Bufala is a fresh cheese that is a true gem of Neapolitan cuisine. It is made from the milk of water buffaloes and is known for its soft, creamy texture and delicate flavor. Neapolitans take great pride in their mozzarella di bufala, using it in various dishes such as Caprese salad, pizza, and panini. The cheese's freshness and quality are key to its exceptional taste.

## *Sfogliatella*

Sfogliatella is a traditional Neapolitan pastry that delights both locals and visitors. This flaky, shell-shaped pastry is filled with a sweet and fragrant ricotta-based filling, often flavored with citrus zest and cinnamon. Sfogliatella can be enjoyed in two variations: "sfogliatella riccia," which has a layered and flaky crust, and "sfogliatella frolla," which has a softer, cookie-like crust. It is a true indulgence for those with a sweet tooth.

Neapolitan cuisine encompasses a wide range of other delicious dishes, including seafood specialties like spaghetti alle vongole (spaghetti with clams), frittura di paranza (mixed fried seafood), and cuoppo napoletano (fried fish served in a paper cone). The use of locally sourced ingredients, such as fresh seafood, tomatoes, and aromatic herbs, adds an authentic and distinctive touch to Neapolitan dishes.

In conclusion, exploring the savory delights of Neapolitan cuisine is a journey that unveils the city's culinary treasures. From the iconic Neapolitan pizza to the comforting Pasta alla Genovese, the exquisite Mozzarella di Bufala, and the indulgent Sfogliatella, each dish reflects the passion, tradition, and flavors that make Neapolitan cuisine truly remarkable. By savoring these classic Neapolitan dishes, you will immerse yourself in the culinary heritage and vibrant gastronomic scene of Naples.

## *Traditional Markets and Food Halls*

### *Mercato di Porta Nolana*

Located in the heart of Naples, Mercato di Porta Nolana is a bustling traditional market that offers a vibrant and authentic shopping experience. With its origins dating back to the 19th century, this market has been a gathering place for locals seeking fresh produce, seafood, meats, and a variety of other products. As you stroll through the market's lively aisles, you'll be captivated by the colorful displays of fruits, vegetables, and aromatic herbs, creating a sensory feast for the eyes and nose. The market is particularly famous for its seafood section, where you can find an abundance of fish, shellfish, and crustaceans brought in fresh from the nearby Gulf of Naples. Engage with the friendly vendors, who are always ready to share their knowledge and recommendations, and discover the authentic flavors of Naples as you immerse yourself in this vibrant market.

## *Mercato di Pignasecca*

Nestled in the heart of the historic center, Mercato di Pignasecca is another treasure among Naples' traditional markets. With a history dating back centuries, this market has been a hub for locals to purchase fresh produce, dairy products, spices, and more. As you explore its narrow alleys, you'll be greeted by stalls overflowing with vibrant fruits, aromatic herbs, and an array of local specialties. The market offers a glimpse into the daily life of Neapolitans, where you can observe the lively interactions between shoppers and vendors. Take the opportunity to taste seasonal fruits and sample local delicacies, such as buffalo mozzarella, sun-dried tomatoes, and Neapolitan pastries. Mercato di Pignasecca is a true gem that allows you to experience the authentic flavors and cultural richness of Naples.

## *La Pignasecca Food Hall*

Adjacent to Mercato di Pignasecca, La Pignasecca Food Hall offers a modern twist on the traditional market experience. This vibrant culinary destination brings together a variety of food stalls and eateries under one roof, offering a diverse selection of gastronomic delights. From freshly prepared street food and artisanal cheese and cured meats to Neapolitan pastries and gelato, you'll find a wide range of flavors to tantalize your taste buds. The food hall provides a dynamic atmosphere where you can savor different culinary creations, mingle with locals, and immerse yourself in the gastronomic culture of Naples. Whether you're looking for a quick bite or a leisurely meal, La Pignasecca Food Hall is a must-visit destination for food enthusiasts.

Visiting traditional markets and food halls like Mercato di Porta Nolana, Mercato di Pignasecca, and La Pignasecca Food Hall allows you to experience the vibrant soul of Naples' culinary scene. These bustling hubs showcase the freshest ingredients, the passionate craftsmanship of local producers, and the rich culinary traditions that have shaped Neapolitan cuisine. Exploring these markets offers an opportunity to engage with the city's vibrant food culture, taste authentic flavors, and discover the true essence of Naples.

## Best Trattorias and Restaurants

### *Authentic Neapolitan Dining Experiences*

Naples is renowned for its vibrant culinary scene, and exploring the city's trattorias and restaurants is a delightful way to immerse yourself in the local gastronomy. Whether you're seeking traditional Neapolitan dishes or innovative culinary creations, the city offers a wide range of dining options to suit every palate. From family-run trattorias with time-honored recipes to upscale restaurants pushing the boundaries of culinary excellence, Naples has it all. Each establishment has its own unique charm, providing a warm and inviting atmosphere where you can enjoy a truly authentic dining experience and savor the flavors that have defined Neapolitan cuisine for centuries.

## *Seafood Specialties*

Given its coastal location, Naples is a haven for seafood lovers. The city's trattorias and restaurants excel in serving fresh and flavorful seafood dishes that showcase the region's bounty from the Mediterranean Sea. From succulent grilled fish and seafood risotto to mouthwatering spaghetti alle vongole (clam pasta) and frittura di paranza (mixed fried seafood), the seafood specialties of Naples are a must-try for any visitor. Many establishments pride themselves on sourcing the finest local catch, ensuring that each dish is a celebration of the sea's flavors and a testament to Naples' rich maritime heritage.

## Vegetarian and Vegan Options

Naples also caters to those with vegetarian and vegan preferences, offering a diverse selection of plant-based dishes that showcase the city's culinary creativity. Trattorias and restaurants have embraced the growing demand for vegetarian and vegan options, ensuring that everyone can enjoy a satisfying and flavorful meal. From hearty pasta dishes with fresh vegetables to innovative plant-based creations inspired by traditional Neapolitan recipes, there is no shortage of options for those seeking vegetarian and vegan delights in Naples.

## Sweet Delights: Pastries and Gelato

No culinary journey in Naples is complete without indulging in the city's sweet delights. Naples is renowned for its mouthwatering pastries and gelato, and numerous pastry shops and gelaterias dot the streets, tempting passersby with their irresistible creations. Sink your teeth into a warm sfogliatella, a delicate pastry filled with sweet ricotta cream and flavored with citrus and cinnamon. Alternatively, savor the creamy richness of a traditional Neapolitan gelato, with flavors ranging from classic vanilla and chocolate to innovative combinations like pistachio and ricotta with candied fruit. These sweet treats are an integral part of Naples' culinary heritage and offer a delightful way to end your dining experience on a high note.

In Naples, the trattorias and restaurants not only provide delicious meals but also offer a glimpse into the city's vibrant culinary culture. Whether you're indulging in seafood specialties, exploring vegetarian and vegan options, or satisfying your sweet tooth with pastries and gelato, Naples' dining scene is sure to leave a lasting impression. Embrace the city's culinary treasures and embark on a gastronomic adventure that will tantalize your taste buds and create lasting memories.

# CHAPTER 7

## Beyond Naples: Day Trips and Excursions

### *The Amalfi Coast*

Located just a short distance from Naples, the Amalfi Coast is a breathtaking stretch of coastline renowned for its stunning natural beauty, charming cliffside villages, and rich historical heritage. A day trip to the Amalfi Coast is an opportunity to immerse yourself in the enchanting allure of this UNESCO World Heritage site and experience the magic of Positano, Amalfi, and Ravello.

The Amalfi Coast is situated along the southern edge of the Sorrentine Peninsula in the Campania region of Italy. To reach the Amalfi Coast from Naples, you can take various transportation options. One popular choice is to travel by road, either by renting a car or taking a bus along the scenic coastal road known as the SS163. This picturesque route offers panoramic views of the coastline and takes you through the charming towns that dot the landscape. Alternatively, you can opt for a ferry or boat ride from Naples, which allows you to admire the coast from the sea and adds a touch of romance to your journey.

## *Positano*

As you arrive on the Amalfi Coast, the first stop on your day trip is Positano. This iconic village is nestled on the cliffs overlooking the crystal-clear waters of the Mediterranean Sea. With its pastel-colored houses, narrow streets, and cascading flowers, Positano exudes a unique charm that has attracted artists, writers, and travelers for centuries. Take a leisurely stroll along the winding streets, explore the boutique shops selling locally crafted ceramics and fashion, and savor the delicious cuisine in one of the many seaside restaurants. Don't miss the opportunity to relax on the beautiful Spiaggia Grande beach or take a boat tour to discover hidden coves and secluded beaches along the coast.

## *Amalfi*

Continuing your journey along the coast, you'll reach the town of Amalfi, which once served as a powerful maritime republic during the Middle Ages. This historic town is characterized by its grand cathedral, known as the Duomo di Amalfi, which dominates the main square. Visit the cathedral to admire its intricate architecture and the relics of St. Andrew, the town's patron saint. Take a stroll through the narrow alleys lined with shops selling local products, including the famous limoncello liqueur made from the region's abundant lemons. While in Amalfi, you can also explore the Museum of Paper, which showcases the town's traditional paper-making craft.

## *Ravello*

The final stop on your day trip is the picturesque town of Ravello, perched high above the Amalfi Coast. Ravello offers breathtaking views of the coastline and the opportunity to immerse yourself in its rich cultural heritage. Visit the Villa Rufolo, an ancient mansion surrounded by beautiful gardens that inspired Richard Wagner's opera "Parsifal." Attend a concert at the stunning cliffside auditorium of the Villa Cimbrone, which hosts world-class performances amidst an awe-inspiring setting. Ravello is also known for its vibrant arts scene, with numerous galleries showcasing the works of local and international artists.

The Amalfi Coast has a long and storied history that dates back to ancient times. Its strategic location made it a hub of trade and cultural exchange, resulting in the development of a unique architectural style known as Amalfi Romanesque. The region's maritime heritage is evident in the charming fishing villages and the iconic "sailing ship" architectural elements found in churches and buildings. The Amalfi Coast's cultural significance extends beyond its architectural beauty. It has served as a source of inspiration for artists and writers, including musicians like Wagner and authors like John Steinbeck, who famously described the region as a place of "dreamlike enchantment."

Embarking on a day trip to the Amalfi Coast is an opportunity to immerse yourself in the captivating beauty and rich history of this extraordinary destination. From the charm of Positano to the historical significance of Amalfi and the artistic allure of Ravello, each stop along the coast offers a unique experience that will leave you with cherished memories and a deeper appreciation for the cultural legacy of the Amalfi Coast civilization.

## *Pompeii and Herculaneum*

Located near Naples, the ancient Roman cities of Pompeii and Herculaneum offer a unique glimpse into the daily life, architecture, and culture of the Roman Empire. Buried under volcanic ash and preserved for centuries, these archaeological sites provide an extraordinary opportunity to step back in time and witness the grandeur and tragedy of ancient Pompeii and Herculaneum civilizations.

Pompeii and Herculaneum are both situated in the region of Campania, near the city of Naples. To reach these remarkable archaeological sites, you can easily take a train from Naples to the respective stations: Pompei Scavi - Villa dei Misteri for Pompeii and Ercolano Scavi for Herculaneum. Both sites are well-connected by public transportation, making them easily accessible for day trips from Naples.

## *Pompeii Archaeological Park*

Pompeii was a thriving Roman city until it was tragically buried under the volcanic ash of Mount

Vesuvius during the eruption in 79 AD. Rediscovered in the 18th century, the archaeological site of Pompeii is now an open-air museum that offers a fascinating insight into the daily life of ancient Romans. As you explore the remarkably preserved streets, houses, and public buildings, you'll witness the splendor of the ancient city, including its amphitheater, forum, and impressive villas. Don't miss the famous plaster casts of the volcano's victims, which provide haunting glimpses into the final moments of Pompeii's inhabitants.

## *Herculaneum Archaeological Park*

Located just a few kilometers from Pompeii, Herculaneum was also buried during the eruption of Mount Vesuvius. However, unlike Pompeii, Herculaneum was preserved by layers of volcanic mud, resulting in an astonishing level of preservation. The archaeological site of Herculaneum allows visitors to explore the remarkably well-preserved houses, shops, and public buildings. Walk along the ancient streets, marvel at the intricate mosaics and frescoes adorning the walls, and discover the thermal baths that were an integral part of Roman society. Herculaneum provides a more intimate and immersive experience, offering a glimpse into the daily lives of its inhabitants.

Exploring Pompeii and Herculaneum provides valuable insights into the social and cultural dynamics of ancient Roman society. These cities were vibrant centers of trade, art, and intellectual pursuits, and their ruins offer a fascinating window into the daily lives and customs of the ancient inhabitants. From the grandeur of the public buildings to the intricate details of the private residences, the ruins reflect the wealth, taste, and social hierarchies of the ancient Pompeii and Herculaneum civilizations. The preserved artifacts, such as statues, household items, and artwork, further enhance our understanding of the daily rituals, religious beliefs, and artistic expressions of the time.

Visiting Pompeii and Herculaneum allows us to connect with the past and appreciate the resilience of these ancient civilizations in the face of natural disaster. It is a testament to the enduring legacy of the Roman Empire and a reminder of the fragile nature of human existence. As you explore these extraordinary archaeological sites, you will be transported back in time, walking in the footsteps of those who lived and thrived in these ancient cities, until they were forever frozen in the shadow of Mount Vesuvius.

## Mount Vesuvius

Rising majestically above the Bay of Naples, Mount Vesuvius stands as a silent witness to one of the most significant volcanic eruptions in history. A visit to this iconic volcano offers an exhilarating opportunity to hike to the summit, delve into its rich history and geology, and gain a deeper understanding of the profound impact it had on ancient civilizations.

Mount Vesuvius is located in the Campania region, just a short distance from Naples. To reach the volcano, you can take a combination of public transportation and guided tours. From Naples, you can travel by train or bus to the town of Pompei Scavi - Villa dei Misteri. From there, you can join a guided tour or take a shuttle bus that will transport you to the base of Mount Vesuvius. It is recommended to book a guided tour to ensure a safe and informative experience.

### Hiking to the Summit

The highlight of visiting Mount Vesuvius is the opportunity to hike to the summit and stand at the edge of the volcanic crater. The trail winds its way through the volcanic landscape, offering panoramic views of the surrounding countryside, the Bay of

Naples, and the city of Naples itself. As you ascend, you'll witness the dramatic change in vegetation, from lush greenery to barren volcanic ash. The hike is moderately challenging, but the reward of reaching the summit is truly breathtaking. Standing atop Mount Vesuvius and peering into the crater is a humbling experience that will leave you in awe of the immense power of nature.

## *History and Geology*

Mount Vesuvius is infamous for its catastrophic eruption in 79 AD, which buried the cities of Pompeii and Herculaneum under layers of ash and pumice. This event, although devastating, resulted in the preservation of these ancient Roman cities, providing invaluable insights into daily life during the Roman Empire. The volcano has a long history of eruptions, with documented activity dating back thousands of years. Its unique geology and volcanic nature make it a subject of fascination for scientists and geologists who study its behavior and monitor its activity to this day.

Mount Vesuvius holds immense social and cultural significance, both historically and in the present day. The eruption of 79 AD left a lasting impact on ancient Roman civilization, forever freezing a moment in time. The preserved ruins of Pompeii and Herculaneum provide a glimpse into the lives of the people who lived in the shadow of the volcano. Today, the volcano's iconic silhouette and its turbulent history serve as a reminder of the fragility of human existence and the awe-inspiring power of nature. The ongoing scientific study of Mount Vesuvius contributes to our understanding of volcanic activity and helps protect the local communities that live in its vicinity.

Visiting Mount Vesuvius offers a unique and thrilling experience that combines adventure, history, and natural beauty. It allows you to immerse yourself in the fascinating world of volcanoes, witness the scars of past eruptions, and appreciate the resilience of ancient civilizations. As you hike to the summit and take in the awe-inspiring views, you will be reminded of the captivating and ever-changing forces that have shaped the landscape and the human story throughout the centuries.

# CHAPTER 8

## Practical Information and Tips

### *Accommodation Options in Naples*

When planning a trip to Naples, it's essential to consider your accommodation options. The city offers a range of choices, including hotels, bed and breakfasts, and apartments, each offering a unique experience and a chance to immerse yourself in the captivating aspect of ancient Naples civilization. Here are some considerations and recommendations to help you find the perfect place to stay.

**Hotels**
Naples boasts a wide selection of hotels catering to various budgets and preferences. From luxury accommodations to boutique hotels and budget-friendly options, there is something for every traveler. Many hotels are conveniently located in the city center, offering easy access to popular attractions, dining establishments, and shopping districts.

Considerations when choosing a hotel in Naples include its proximity to public transportation, such as metro stations and bus stops, as well as its accessibility to the main tourist sites. It's advisable to read reviews and check amenities offered, such as Wi-Fi, air conditioning, and breakfast options, to ensure a comfortable stay.

## *Bed and Breakfasts*

For a more intimate and personalized experience, consider staying in a bed and breakfast (B&B). Naples is known for its charming B&Bs that provide a cozy atmosphere and attentive service. These accommodations are often located in historic buildings and offer a glimpse into the local culture and hospitality.

B&Bs can be found in various neighborhoods throughout Naples, allowing you to choose a location that suits your preferences. Whether you prefer to stay in the bustling city center or in a quieter residential area, there are bed and breakfasts to cater to your needs.

## *Apartments*

Renting an apartment in Naples is an excellent option for those seeking a more independent and home-like experience. Apartments provide the flexibility of self-catering and the opportunity to live like a local. They are particularly suitable for families or longer stays, as they often come equipped with kitchens and multiple bedrooms.

Naples offers a wide range of apartments available for short-term rentals. They can be found in different neighborhoods, allowing you to choose a location that aligns with your interests and preferences. It's advisable to research reputable rental agencies and read reviews to ensure a smooth and enjoyable experience.

## *Neighborhood Recommendations*

When selecting your accommodation in Naples, it's worth considering the different neighborhoods and their unique characteristics. Here are a few recommendations:

***Historic Center (Centro Storico):*** This is the heart of Naples and an ideal location for those interested in exploring the city's historic sites, museums, and vibrant street life. Staying in the Historic Center puts you in close proximity to popular attractions like the San Carlo Theater, Piazza del Plebiscito, and Spaccanapoli.

***Chiaia***: Located along the waterfront, Chiaia offers a more upscale and elegant atmosphere. It is known for its high-end boutiques, restaurants, and panoramic views of the bay. Chiaia is a great choice for those seeking a quieter and more refined stay.

*Vomero*: Perched on a hill overlooking the city, Vomero offers stunning views and a more residential feel. It is known for its shopping streets, lively piazzas, and the iconic Castel Sant'Elmo. Vomero is well-connected to the city center via the funicular railway and offers a tranquil retreat from the bustling city below.

Naples offers a diverse range of accommodation options to suit every traveler's needs. Whether you choose a hotel in the city center, a charming bed and breakfast, or a self-catering apartment, each option provides an opportunity to immerse yourself in the captivating aspect of ancient Naples civilization. By considering the location, amenities, and neighborhood preferences, you can find the perfect place to stay and make the most of your visit to this vibrant city.

## *Getting Around Naples*

Naples, with its rich history and vibrant culture, offers various transportation options to help you navigate the city and explore its captivating aspects of ancient Naples civilization. Whether you prefer public transportation, taxis, or car rentals, here is some comprehensive information and tips to assist you in getting around Naples.

***Public Transportation***
Naples has an extensive public transportation system that includes buses, trams, metro lines, and funicular railways, making it convenient to move around the city. Here are the main modes of public transportation:

***Buses***: The bus network in Naples covers the entire city, including the suburbs. It's a cost-effective way to reach different neighborhoods and attractions. Tickets can be purchased at newsstands, tobacco shops, or onboard the bus.

***Metro***: The metro system in Naples consists of Line 1 (Linea 1) and Line 2 (Linea 2). Line 1 connects the city center with areas like Vomero, while Line 2 connects the central train station (Napoli Centrale) with neighborhoods like Chiaia and Mergellina. Metro tickets can be purchased at metro stations.

***Funiculars***: Naples is known for its funicular railways, which provide scenic and convenient access to elevated neighborhoods. The three funicular lines are Centrale-Montesanto, Centrale-Chiaia, and Mergellina. These are a great way to reach Vomero, Chiaia, and other hillside areas.

*Taxis*:

Taxis are readily available in Naples, and they offer a convenient way to get around the city, especially if you're carrying luggage or prefer a more direct mode of transportation. Taxis can be hailed on the street, found at designated taxi stands, or booked through a taxi app. It's important to ensure the taxi has a working meter or negotiate the fare before starting your journey.

*Car Rentals:*

Renting a car in Naples gives you the flexibility to explore the city and its surrounding areas at your own pace. However, it's worth noting that traffic in Naples can be challenging, especially in the city center, due to narrow streets and limited parking spaces. It's recommended to choose a hotel with parking facilities or opt for public parking garages if you decide to rent a car.

Naples offers a range of transportation options to suit different preferences and needs. Whether you choose public transportation for convenience and affordability, taxis for a more direct journey, or car rentals for flexibility, each mode of transportation allows you to explore the captivating aspects of ancient Naples civilization. By considering the location, traffic conditions, and specific requirements, you can navigate the city with ease and make the most of your time in Naples.

## *Safety Tips and Local Customs in Naples*

When visiting Naples, it's important to be aware of safety precautions and local customs to ensure a pleasant and enjoyable experience. Here are some valuable tips to enhance your stay in this captivating city, along with useful Italian phrases and words, recommended itineraries, and information about festivals and events.

### Safety Tips

***Stay Vigilant***: Like in any urban environment, it's advisable to remain vigilant and take precautions to protect your belongings. Keep an eye on your personal belongings, especially in crowded areas and public transportation.

***Use Secure Transportation:*** When using public transportation or taxis, ensure you choose licensed and reputable services. Be cautious of unofficial taxis, especially those without meters or fixed rates.

***Be Mindful of Pickpockets***: Naples, like many tourist destinations, can attract pickpockets. Keep your valuables secure, avoid displaying expensive items, and be aware of your surroundings, particularly in crowded places, markets, and popular tourist sites.

***Respect Local Customs***: Naples has a rich cultural heritage, and it's important to respect local customs and traditions. Dress modestly when visiting religious sites, and be mindful of local customs and social norms.

## *Local Customs and Useful Phrases*

***Greetings***: "Buongiorno" (Good morning/Good day) and "Buonasera" (Good evening) are commonly used greetings in Naples. "Grazie" (Thank you) and "Prego" (You're welcome) are polite expressions to use when interacting with locals.

***Language***: While English is spoken in many tourist areas, learning a few basic Italian phrases can enhance your interactions with locals. "Scusa" (Excuse me), "Per favore" (Please), and "Mi scusi"

(Excuse me, formal) are useful phrases for everyday conversations.

***Ordering Food***: When dining out, it's customary to greet the waiter with "Buonasera" and conclude your meal with "Il conto, per favore" (The bill, please). Don't forget to try some local specialties like pizza, pasta, and sfogliatella!

## *Recommended Itineraries*

***One Day***: Start with a visit to the historic center, exploring landmarks like Spaccanapoli and San Gregorio Armeno. Enjoy a pizza lunch and visit the Naples National Archaeological Museum or the Royal Palace. Conclude the day with a stroll along the seafront promenade, Via Caracciolo.

***Two to Three Days***: Day one can include the above itinerary along with a trip to Mount Vesuvius or the ancient ruins of Pompeii. On day two, explore the vibrant neighborhoods of Chiaia and Vomero, visit Castel Sant'Elmo, and enjoy panoramic views of the city. Consider a day trip to the enchanting Amalfi Coast on day three.

## Festivals and Events

Naples hosts numerous festivals and events throughout the year, showcasing its rich cultural heritage. Here are a few notable ones:

***Pizza Village***: Held in June, this festival celebrates Naples' famous pizza with various vendors and activities dedicated to the art of pizza-making.

***San Gennaro Feast***: Taking place in September, this religious festival honors the patron saint of Naples, San Gennaro, with processions, music, and traditional ceremonies.

***Christmas Alley***: During the holiday season, the streets of Naples come alive with lights, decorations, and markets offering traditional Christmas treats and crafts.

Naples offers a wealth of cultural experiences, but it's essential to prioritize safety, respect local customs, and familiarize yourself with useful Italian phrases. By following these tips, you can make the most

# Conclusion

Exploring Naples is an enriching experience that offers a captivating blend of history, art, culture, and culinary delights. From the magnificent churches and cathedrals to the fascinating museums and art galleries, Naples is a city that breathes life into its ancient civilization.

The churches and cathedrals of Naples, such as Duomo di San Gennaro, Basilica di Santa Chiara, San Domenico Maggiore, and Gesù Nuovo Church, are not only architectural wonders but also repositories of religious and cultural significance. They showcase the city's deep-rooted religious traditions and provide a glimpse into the artistic mastery of the past.

The museums and art galleries of Naples, including the Naples National Archaeological Museum, Museo di Capodimonte, Museo Cappella Sansevero, and MADRE Contemporary Art Museum, house invaluable treasures that reflect the city's historical, artistic, and cultural heritage. They offer a journey through time, allowing visitors to connect with ancient civilizations, renowned artists, and contemporary art movements.

Exploring the neighborhoods and districts of Naples, such as Spaccanapoli, Quartieri Spagnoli, Vomero, and Chiaia, unveils the city's vibrant street life, local traditions, and distinctive character. Each neighborhood has its own charm, from the narrow alleys and lively markets to the elegant streets and panoramic views.

Delving into Neapolitan cuisine reveals a world of savory delights, including classic dishes like Neapolitan pizza, pasta alla Genovese, mozzarella di bufala, and sfogliatella. These culinary creations are deeply rooted in local traditions and reflect the rich flavors and ingredients of the region.

Exploring the traditional markets and food halls, such as Mercato di Porta Nolana, Mercato di Pignasecca, and La Pignasecca Food Hall, provides an immersive experience into the local gastronomy. These bustling hubs offer a wide variety of fresh produce, seafood, spices, and traditional Neapolitan delicacies.

Indulging in the best trattorias and restaurants in Naples allows visitors to savor authentic Neapolitan dining experiences. From seafood specialties to vegetarian and vegan options, the city's culinary scene caters to diverse preferences. And of course, no visit to Naples is complete without indulging in sweet delights like pastries and gelato, which showcase the city's mastery of dessert-making.

Venturing beyond Naples on day trips and excursions reveals the breathtaking beauty of the Amalfi Coast, the ancient ruins of Pompeii and Herculaneum, and the majestic Mount Vesuvius. These destinations offer insights into ancient civilizations, geological wonders, and stunning landscapes that have captivated travelers for centuries.

Understanding the practical information and tips for exploring Naples, including accommodation options, getting around the city, and being aware of safety precautions and local customs, ensures a smooth and enjoyable visit.

Naples is a city that embraces its past while embracing the present. Its vibrant festivals and events, like the San Gennaro Feast and Pizza Village, showcase the city's lively spirit and provide opportunities to engage with local traditions and celebrations.

Naples is a city that offers a captivating blend of history, art, culture, culinary delights, and breathtaking landscapes. It invites visitors to immerse themselves in its ancient civilization, discover its hidden gems, and create unforgettable memories.

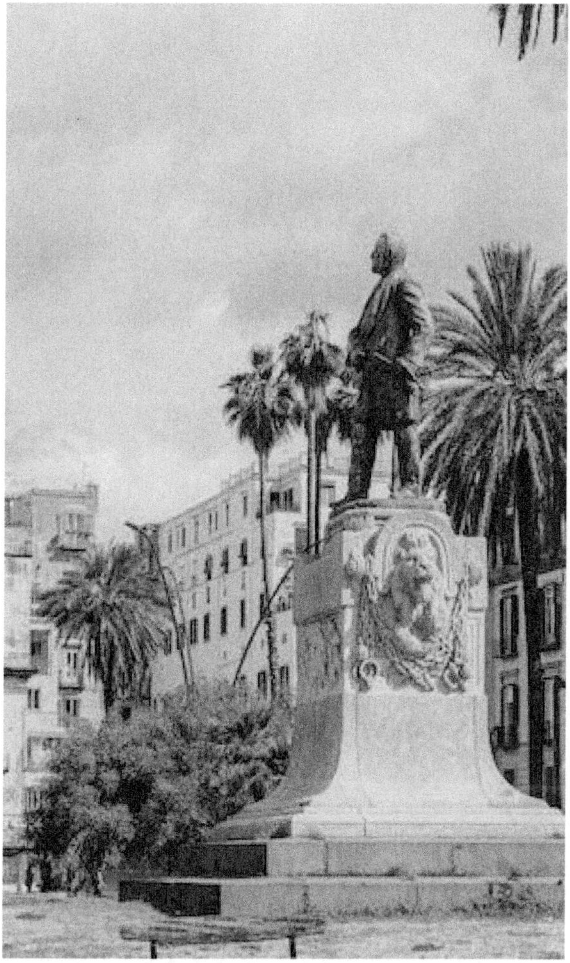

Printed in Great Britain
by Amazon